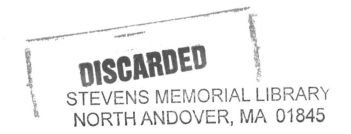

Malala Yousafzai

Education Activist

by Grace Hansen

ABDO
HISTORY MAKER BIOGRAPHIES
Kids

abdopublishing.com

Published by Abdo Kids, a division of ABDO, PO Box 398166, Minneapolis, Minnesota 55439.

Printed in the United States of America, North Mankato, Minnesota.

102014

012015

THIS BOOK CONTAINS RECYCLED MATERIALS

Photo Credits: AP Images, Corbis, Getty Images, iStock, Shutterstock, © User:Alakazou1978 / CC-SA-3.0 p.5, 7, © User:Ziegler175 / CC-SA-3.0 p.5

Production Contributors: Teddy Borth, Jennie Forsberg, Grace Hansen

Design Contributors: Laura Rask, Dorothy Toth

Library of Congress Control Number: 2014943708

Cataloging-in-Publication Data

Hansen, Grace.
 Malala Yousafzai: education activist / Grace Hansen.
   p. cm. -- (History maker biographies)
Includes index.
ISBN 978-1-62970-703-7

1. Yousafzai, Malala, 1997- --Juvenile literature. 2. Youth--Political activity --Pakistan --Biography--Juvenile literature. 3. Social justice--Pakistan--Biography --Juvenile literature. 4. Social justice--Study and teaching--Juvenile literature. 1. Title.

371.822095491--dc23

[B]

2014943708

Table of Contents

Birth

Malala Yousafzai was born on July 12, 1997. She was born in Mingora, Pakistan.

Europ

Afric

Asia

Pakistan

Pakistani Tradition

Usually, Pakistani boys have more schooling. Malala's father wanted girls to have the same.

6

Education for All

Malala's father opened his own school. He let boys and girls attend. Malala went there too.

The **Taliban** took control of Mingora in 2008. It took away the few **rights** women had. Women could not work or learn.

Malala spoke out. She talked about life under **Taliban** rule. The Taliban then closed all girls' schools. This made Malala speak out even more.

13

The Attack and Recovery

People everywhere backed Malala. This made the **Taliban** mad. On October 9, 2012, a member of the Taliban shot Malala.

15

Malala was taken to England. It took her months to get better. She and her family stayed in England. It was not safe to go home.

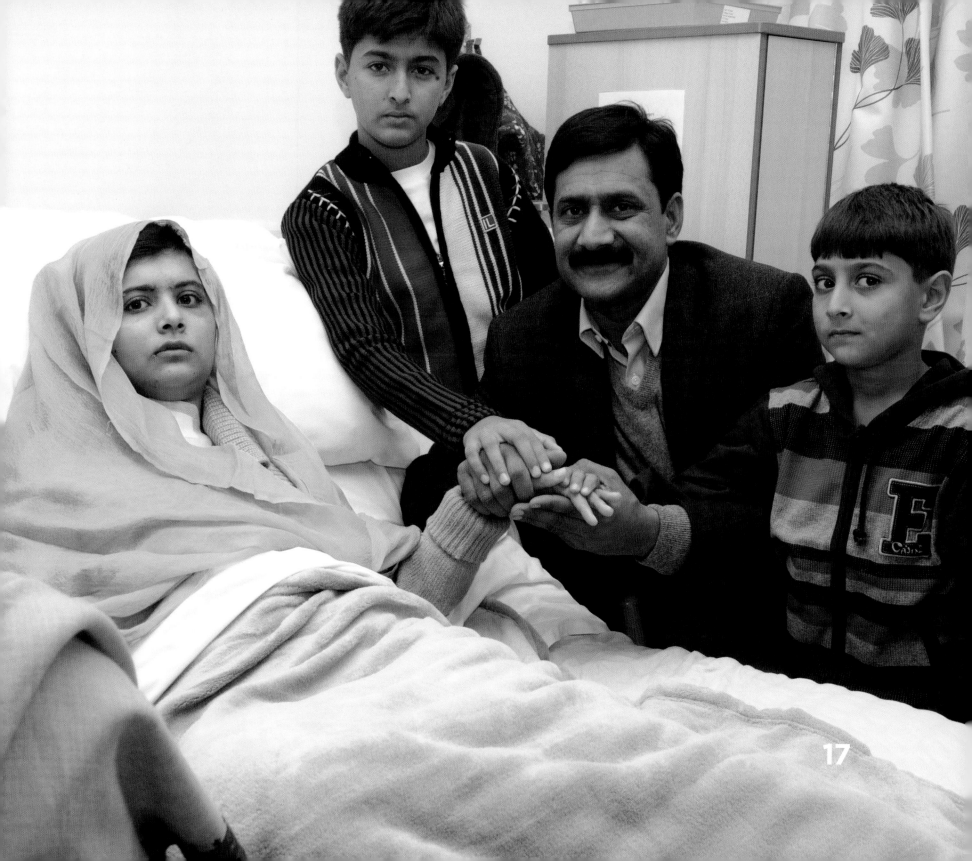

In 2013, Malala spoke at the **United Nations**. She brought attention to global education.

19

Malala Today

Malala still wants education for all. She works to help her country of Pakistan. People **admire** her around the world.

Timeline

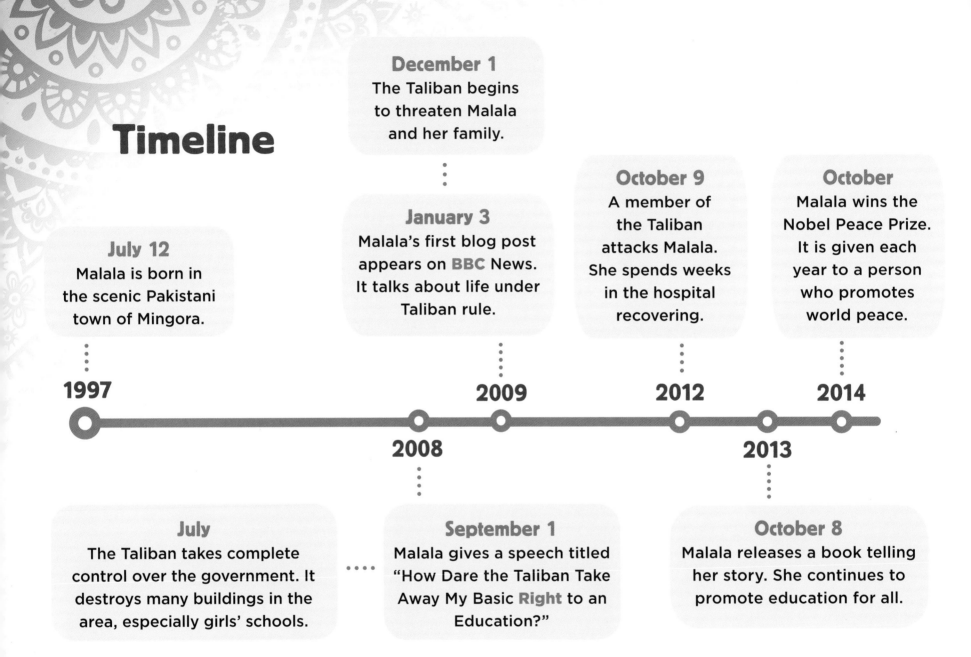

December 1
The Taliban begins to threaten Malala and her family.

January 3
Malala's first blog post appears on **BBC** News. It talks about life under Taliban rule.

October 9
A member of the Taliban attacks Malala. She spends weeks in the hospital recovering.

October
Malala wins the Nobel Peace Prize. It is given each year to a person who promotes world peace.

July 12
Malala is born in the scenic Pakistani town of Mingora.

1997

2009

2012

2014

2008

2013

July
The Taliban takes complete control over the government. It destroys many buildings in the area, especially girls' schools.

September 1
Malala gives a speech titled "How Dare the Taliban Take Away My Basic **Right** to an Education?"

October 8
Malala releases a book telling her story. She continues to promote education for all.

22

Glossary

admire – to respect and approve of someone.

BBC – stands for British Broadcasting Corporation. BBC is a popular news source based in the United Kingdom.

right – what one is able to do under the law.

Taliban – a group of Islamic fundamentalists in Afghanistan. It strictly enforces Islamic law. It is especially harsh toward women.

United Nations – a group made up of most of the world's countries. It was created in 1945 to promote peace, security, and unity.

23

Index

abdokids.com

Use this code to log on to abdokids.com and access crafts, games, videos, and more!

Abdo Kids Code:
HMK7037